Contents

Introduction

This time the Cheshire Cat vanished quite slowly. First its body went, then its legs. Then all of it vanished, and there was only its smile.

'There are a lot of cats without a smile, but a smile without a cat! Now that's very strange!' Alice said.

One hot summer day, Alice and her sister are sitting under a tree. Alice sees a white rabbit and runs after it. The rabbit goes down a rabbit-hole and Alice follows it.

Down the rabbit-hole, everything is different. Alice is in 'Wonderland'. Her size changes all the time. Caterpillars can talk and rabbits have watches. The Queen wants to cut off everybody's head. When the Queen sees the Cheshire Cat, she wants to cut off the Cat's head too. But there's a problem. The Cheshire Cat hasn't got a body ... What strange things happen to Alice, in Wonderland? And how will she get back home again?

Charles Dodgson was born in 1838. He went to Oxford University and then he was a teacher there. He was a quiet man and did not talk to people easily.

He wrote *Alice in Wonderland* in 1865. For him, *Alice in Wonderland* was not an important book, so he did not use his name for the book. He used the name Lewis Carroll. But the book sold very well and it was quickly very famous. At that time, children's books always tried to teach something. Lewis Carroll did not try to teach anything. He only wanted to tell a wonderful story.

Carroll wrote a second story about Alice in 1871. He died in 1898. Today, *Alice in Wonderland* is one of the most famous children's stories in the world.

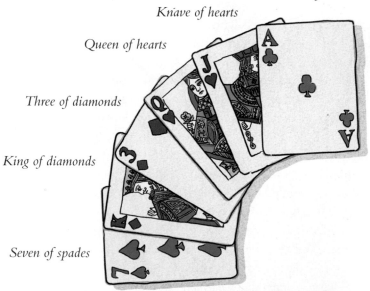

Ace of clubs

Knave of hearts

Queen of hearts

Three of diamonds

King of diamonds

Seven of spades

Chapter 1   Down the Rabbit-hole

Alice and her big sister sat under a tree one sunny day. Alice's sister had a book, but Alice had nothing with her. She looked at her sister's book. There were no pictures or conversations in it.

'Why is she reading a book without pictures or conversations?' she thought. 'I'm bored. I know! I'll look for some flowers.' Then she thought, 'No, it's too hot for that and I feel sleepy.'

Suddenly, a white rabbit ran past her. It took a watch from its jacket and looked at it. 'Oh! Oh! I'm going to be late!' it said.

'That's strange! A rabbit with a watch!' said Alice.

She jumped up and ran after the animal. It ran down a large rabbit-hole, so Alice went down the hole too. She didn't stop and ask, 'How am I going to get out again?'

Alice fell down and down. But she fell very slowly and didn't feel afraid. 'What's going to happen next?' she wondered.

She looked round. There were cupboards in the walls of the rabbit-hole. Some of the cupboards were open, and there were books in them. Sometimes she saw pictures. She looked down, but she couldn't see any light.

Down, down, down. 'When will the hole end?' she wondered. 'Perhaps I'm going to come out in Australia! I'll have to ask the name of the country. "Please, madam, is this Australia or New Zealand?" No, I can't do that. They'll think I'm stupid.'

She thought about her cat, Dinah. 'What's Dinah doing? Will they remember her milk tonight? Oh, Dinah! Why aren't you here with me? Perhaps there's a mouse here and you can eat it!'

◆

'That bottle was not on the table before,' thought Alice.

Suddenly, Alice was at the bottom of the hole. 'That didn't hurt,' she said and sat up quickly. She could see the White Rabbit and she ran after him again. They were in a different rabbit-hole now.

'Oh, my ears and nose!' the White Rabbit cried. 'It's getting very late!'

He ran faster and vanished through another hole. Alice followed him through the hole. Now she was in a very long room. She looked round for the White Rabbit, but she couldn't see him anywhere.

There were four doors in the room, but Alice couldn't open them. Also, she couldn't see the hole anywhere. 'How am I going to get out?' she wondered.

Then she saw a little table. It had a very small key on it.

'Perhaps it will open one of the doors,' she thought. She took the key and tried to open each door with it. But it was no good. The key was too small.

'This key has to open something,' she thought.

Then she saw a very small door about 40 centimetres high. The little key opened it. She put her head down and looked through the door into a beautiful garden. She tried to walk through it, but she was too big. Sadly, she shut the door again and put the key back on the table.

'Why can't I get smaller?' thought Alice. 'This is a very strange place – so perhaps I can.'

She looked at the table. There was a little bottle on it.

'That bottle was *not* on the table before,' thought Alice.

The bottle had 'DRINK ME' on it in large letters. Alice looked at it carefully.

'Is it all right to drink?' she wondered.

'I'll drink a little,' she thought. She had some and it was very nice. So she had some more.

'This feels strange,' said Alice. 'I'm getting smaller and smaller!' After a short time, she was only 25 centimetres high.

'Now I can go through that door,' she thought. She went to the door, but could not open it. The key was on the table. She went back to the table. But Alice was too short and she couldn't get the key. She tried to climb the table legs, but it was too difficult. The little girl sat down and cried.

'Alice! Alice!' she said after some minutes. 'Don't cry. It isn't going to help you. Stop now!'

Then she saw a little box under the table. She opened it. There was a cake inside. On it, she saw the words, 'EAT ME'.

'Yes, I will eat it,' Alice said. 'Perhaps I'll get bigger and then I can get the key. Or perhaps I'll get smaller. Then I can get under the door into the garden.'

She ate some cake.

'Will I go up or down?' she wondered. She felt the top of her head with her hand. But nothing happened – she stayed the same size. So she finished the cake.

Chapter 2   Alice's Tears

'Oh! What's happening?' cried Alice. 'I'm getting taller and taller!' She looked down. 'Goodbye, feet! Who will put your shoes on for you now? *I* can't do it! I'll give you some new shoes for Christmas. I'll have to send them to you!'

In a short time, Alice was more than three metres high.

'I want to go into that garden!' she thought. She took the little key from the table. Then she went to the door and opened it. But she was too big and couldn't go through it.

She sat down and began to cry again. Because she was very big, her tears were very big too.

'Alice, stop it this minute! Don't cry!' she said.

But she couldn't stop the big tears and after a time there was water everywhere.

◆

She heard the sound of small feet. She looked down and there was the White Rabbit again. He had his best clothes on, and in one hand he had a white hat.

'Oh, the Duchess, the Duchess!' he said. 'She'll be angry with me because I'm late!'

Alice wanted to ask him for help. 'Please, Sir – ' she said very politely.

The White Rabbit jumped. He ran out of the room and his hat fell from his hands. Alice took the hat.

'Am I different?' she wondered. 'I was Alice yesterday, but everything is different today. Perhaps I'm not *me* now. So who am I? *That's* the question.'

She began to think about her friends. 'Perhaps I'm one of them,' she thought. 'I'm not Ada because her hair is different to mine. I don't want to be my friend Mabel, because she doesn't know very much. *I* know more than *she* does.' Then she thought, 'Do I know more? Let me see. What's four and four? Eight. Eight and eight is sixteen. Sixteen and sixteen is ... Oh! I can't remember!' And she started to cry again.

But this time her tears were small tears – she was small again! 'Why?' she wondered. Then she understood. She had the White Rabbit's hat in her hand.

'I'm smaller because I've got the hat in my hand!' she thought.

She put the hat on. It was the right size for her head.

'Am I smaller than the table now?' she wondered. She went to the table and stood next to it. She *was* smaller than the table. 'I'm getting smaller all the time!' she cried. 'I'm going to vanish!' She quickly took the hat off.

'Now I can go into the garden!' thought Alice, and she started to run to the little door. But before she got there, she fell into some water. She tried to put her feet on the ground but she couldn't. She had to swim.

'I'm in the sea!' she thought. But it wasn't the sea. The water was her tears.

◆

Something was in the water — Alice could hear it. 'Perhaps it's a big fish or sea animal,' she thought. She looked round. There, very near her, was a mouse.

'I'll speak to it,' thought Alice. 'Everything is strange here. Perhaps it can speak and understand me.'

'Oh Mouse,' she said. 'Do you know the way out of this room?' The Mouse didn't answer.

'Perhaps it doesn't understand English. Perhaps it's a French mouse,' Alice thought. She remembered some words from her schoolbook, so she spoke to the mouse in French.

'Where is my cat?' she asked.

The Mouse moved quickly away from her.

'Oh, I'm sorry,' said Alice. 'I forgot. You're a mouse, so you don't like cats.'

'Don't like cats!' cried the mouse. 'I'm a mouse. Of course I don't like cats!'

'No,' Alice said. 'No. But I think you will like Dinah. She is a nice, dear thing. She's very quiet and good. She catches a mouse every day — Oh! You're angry again! We won't talk about Dinah any more — '

'*We*!' cried the Mouse. 'I *never* speak about cats! Our family hates cats! I don't want to hear any more about them.'

'No, no,' said Alice quickly. 'Perhaps — perhaps you like dogs? There's a very nice little dog near our house. It likes playing with children but it works too. It kills all the m — Oh! I'm sorry!'

The Mouse looked angrily at her and swam quickly away.

'Dear Mouse!' said Alice softly. 'Come back again and we won't talk about cats or dogs.'

When the Mouse heard this, it turned round. It swam slowly back. 'All right,' it said. 'I'll talk to you, but let's get out of the water.'

They climbed out and Alice looked round. There were a lot of animals and birds in the water. When they saw her, they got out of the water too.

Chapter 3   A Race

Alice and the birds and animals felt cold and wet. The largest bird spoke to Alice.

'Good afternoon,' it said loudly. 'I am the Dodo.'

'What is a Dodo?' thought Alice, but she smiled politely. 'Hello, Dodo. I'm Alice,' she said.

'I have an idea,' said the Dodo. 'We all want to get warm. So let's have a race – a Caucus race.'

'What is a Caucus race?' Alice asked.

'I can tell you,' said the Dodo, 'but I won't. I'll show you! That will be easier.'

He put the animals and birds in different places in the room. In a race, somebody usually says, 'One, two, three, go!' But the Dodo didn't do that. Everybody started to run at different times and stopped at different times too. After half an hour, the Dodo cried, 'Everybody stop!' All the birds and animals stopped. Then they all came to the Dodo and stood round it. 'Who was first? Who was first?' they shouted.

The Dodo had to think about it. He sat for a long time with his finger in his mouth. Then he said, 'Everybody was first. So everybody can have a chocolate.'

'What is a Caucus race?' Alice asked.

'But who will give us the chocolates?' the Mouse asked.

'*She* will,' the Dodo said and looked at Alice. The birds and animals came and stood round Alice.

'Chocolates, chocolates!' they cried.

'What am I going to do?' thought Alice. 'I haven't got any chocolates.' But then she saw a box of chocolates near her feet.

'Here we are,' she said, and opened the box. There was one chocolate for each bird and animal.

'But Alice has to have something, you know,' said the Mouse.

'Of course,' the Dodo answered. He turned to Alice. 'What can *you* have?' he asked.

'I can have the box,' said Alice sadly.

'Give it to me,' said the Dodo and Alice gave it to him.

They all stood round Alice again, and the Dodo gave her the box.

'Please take this beautiful box,' he said.

'This is very stupid,' thought Alice and she wanted to laugh. But she didn't. She took the box and smiled politely.

◆

The animals and birds ate their chocolates noisily. Some of them cried. The big animals and birds wanted more. But the chocolates were too big for the small birds, and they had to eat them very slowly. When they finished their chocolates, they sat and looked at Alice.

'Oh, where is Dinah?' said Alice. 'I want her with me.'

'And who is Dinah?' the Dodo asked.

Alice loved to talk about her cat. 'Dinah's our cat. She's very nice. And very clever and fast. She can catch a mouse in the morning for her breakfast and a little bird in the evening for her dinner – Oh! I'm sorry!'

It was too late. The birds and animals started leaving.

One old bird said, 'I really have to go home. It gets so cold at night!'

Another bird called to her children, 'Come away, my dears! It's time for bed!'

They all spoke politely to Alice and left the room.

'Oh, why did I talk about Dinah?' cried Alice. 'Nobody likes Dinah down here, but she's the best cat in the world. Perhaps I'll never see her again!'

She sat down and started to cry again. After a time, she heard the sound of small feet and looked up.

'Perhaps it's the Mouse,' she thought.

Chapter 4   The White Rabbit's House

It was not the Mouse. It was the White Rabbit. He came slowly into the room.

'Oh, my ears and nose!' he said quietly. 'The Duchess! The Duchess! She'll be angry! They'll cut off my head, I know! Oh, where is it? Where did it fall?'

'He's looking for his hat,' thought Alice.

She wanted to help him, but she couldn't see the hat anywhere. She looked round. Everything was different now. She wasn't in the long room any more, and there was no table or water. She was outside again, in the country.

The White Rabbit saw her. 'What *are* you doing out here, Mary Ann?' he asked angrily. 'Run home this minute and bring me a hat. Quick, now!'

◆

Alice didn't say, 'I'm not Mary Ann.' She felt too afraid. She ran fast and after a short time, she came to a pretty little house. Above the door were the words 'W. RABBIT'. She went in and ran up the stairs.

'This is very strange,' she thought. 'I hope I don't meet Mary Ann. Why am I bringing a rabbit his hat? Perhaps when I get home, I'll do things for Dinah. Perhaps I'll watch mouse-holes for her!'

She went into a small room. There, on a table, was a hat and a little bottle. Alice took the hat and looked at the bottle. It didn't have the words 'DRINK ME' on it, but she drank from it.

'I know *something* interesting will happen,' she thought. 'When I eat or drink something here, it always does. I hope I get bigger this time. I don't like being small.'

She drank half the bottle. 'Oh, I'm getting much taller!' she cried. 'Oh!' Her head hit the top of the house and she put the bottle down quickly.

'Oh no!' she thought. 'I hope I don't get taller!'

She sat down. But after a very short time she was too big for the room. She had to put one arm out of the window and one foot in the fireplace.

'I can't do any more,' she thought. 'What *will* happen to me?'

She waited for some time, but she didn't get bigger.

'Well, that's good,' she thought. But then she tried to move and couldn't. She didn't feel well and she was very unhappy.

'I'm never going to get out of here,' she thought. 'It was much nicer at home. First I get larger, then I get smaller, then larger . . . Oh, why did I go down the rabbit-hole? But it *is* interesting here. Perhaps somebody will write a book about this place – and about me! Perhaps *I* will, when I'm bigger.' Then she remembered. 'But I'm bigger now!'

She heard somebody outside. 'Mary Ann, Mary Ann! Where are you? Bring me my hat!' The words came from the garden, outside the window. It was the White Rabbit.

◆

He came inside and ran up the stairs to the room. He tried to open the door. But he couldn't because Alice's back was next to it.

'I'll climb in through the window,' the Rabbit said.

'Oh no, you won't,' thought Alice. She waited and listened. One of her arms was outside the window. When she could hear the Rabbit outside the window, she moved her arm up and down. There was a little cry.

'Pat, Pat, where are you? Come here!' shouted the Rabbit.

'Coming, Sir,' somebody – or something – answered.

'What's that in the window?' asked the Rabbit.

'It's an arm, Sir,' Pat answered.

'Don't be stupid! How can it be an arm? It's too big!'

'It is very big, but it is an arm, sir.'

'Well, what's it doing up there? Take it away!' said the Rabbit angrily.

Alice moved her arm again. Now there were two little cries. Everything was quiet for a short time, then something hard hit her arm.

'That hurt!' said Alice.

Something came through the window and fell on the floor. Alice looked down. It was a little cake.

'A cake? Why did they throw a cake?' she wondered.

Then she thought, 'I'll eat it and perhaps I'll get smaller again. I *can't* get bigger!' So she ate the cake and two or three minutes later she was small again. She ran out of the house as quickly as she could.

The White Rabbit saw her. He ran after her but Alice ran too fast for him. After some time, she came to a wood. She was tired because she was very small now.

'I have to get bigger again,' said Alice. 'But how? I have to eat or drink something, but the question is – what?'

That *was* the question. She looked all round her, but she couldn't see anything with 'EAT ME' or 'DRINK ME' on it. There were some mushrooms near her. Some were white and some were brown.

'I eat mushrooms for dinner,' she thought. 'I'll eat some mushrooms and perhaps I'll get bigger again.'

One white mushroom was as big as Alice. She stood up tall and looked over the top. There, on top of the mushroom, was a large green caterpillar.

Chapter 5   The Caterpillar

The Caterpillar looked at Alice for some time before it spoke. Then it said slowly, 'Who are you?'

It was a difficult question. 'I ... I don't really know, Sir,' Alice said. 'I was Alice when I got up this morning. But then I changed – and then I changed again – and again.'

'What do you mean?' the Caterpillar asked.

'I don't know,' Alice answered. 'You see, I'm not *me* now.'

'I don't understand,' said the Caterpillar.

'I'll try and tell you,' said Alice. 'You see, I change all the time. It's very difficult for me.'

'Why? I can change very easily.'

'Well, perhaps it's not difficult for you, but it is for me,' said Alice.

'For *you*? Who are *you*?' said the Caterpillar and laughed.

Alice felt angry. 'It asked me that question before,' she thought. She stood very tall and said, 'I will tell you, but first, you tell me. Who are you?'

'Why do I have to tell you?' asked the Caterpillar.

This was another difficult question and Alice could not answer it.

'This caterpillar isn't very friendly,' she thought. So she walked away.

◆

The Caterpillar looked at Alice for some time before it spoke.

'Come back!' the Caterpillar called. 'I want to tell you something important.' Alice turned and came back again.

'Don't get angry,' said the Caterpillar.

'Is that all?' Alice asked. She felt *very* angry with the Caterpillar.

'No,' said the Caterpillar.

It did not speak for some minutes, then it said, 'So you're different, are you?'

'Yes, I am, Sir,' said Alice. 'I can't remember things, and my size changes all the time. Sometimes I get bigger and then I get smaller again.'

'So you can't remember things,' said the Caterpillar. 'Try this. Repeat, "You are old, Father William."'

Alice put her hands behind her back and repeated:

'You are old, Father William,' the young man said,
'And your hair is now very white;
So why do you often stand on your head –
Do you think at your age it is right?'

'You are old, Father William,' the young man said,
'You are old and really quite fat;
But you jump up and down and turn round and round,
Now what is the answer to that?'

'That is not right,' said the Caterpillar.

'I know. Some of the words are different,' said Alice.

'It's wrong from beginning to end,' said the Caterpillar. It was quiet for a time. Then it asked, 'What size would you like to be?'

'I'd like to be taller,' said Alice. 'Seven centimetres is too small.'

'Seven centimetres is a very good size,' said the Caterpillar angrily. It stood up very tall.

'It's a good size for you, but not for me,' said Alice. And she thought, 'Why does it get angry all the time?'

The Caterpillar was quiet for some minutes. Then it climbed down the mushroom. 'Eat from *my* mushroom and you'll get bigger. Eat from that brown mushroom there and you'll get smaller,' it said. It started to move away. A minute later, it vanished behind a flower and Alice never saw it again.

◆

Alice looked at the two mushrooms and thought for a minute. Then she went to the Caterpillar's mushroom and broke off some of it with her right hand. She went to the brown mushroom and did the same with her left hand.

She ate some of the brown mushroom. Suddenly, her head hit her foot.

'Oh!' she cried. 'I'm really small!'

She quickly ate a little from the white mushroom in her left hand. She started to get bigger. She ate some more, and got very tall. Then she ate some from one hand and some from the other. In a short time, she was her right size again.

She felt quite strange. 'What shall I do now?' she wondered. 'I know! I'll look for that beautiful garden.'

She began to walk through the wood. After some time, she came to a little house. It was about one metre high.

'I can't go inside, I'm too big,' Alice thought. 'The people in the house will be afraid of me. I know! I'll eat some of the brown mushroom.'

When she was 18 centimetres high, she walked to the house. She opened the door and went in.

Chapter 6 The Duchess and the Cheshire Cat

Inside, a large, ugly woman sat with a baby in her arms. There was a cook by the fire and there was food on the table. Near the fire, there was a large cat with a big smile. This smile went from ear to ear on its face.

'I think that woman is the Duchess,' thought Alice. 'Can girls speak to Duchesses?' she wondered.

But the Duchess did not say anything to her, so Alice asked, 'Please, why is your cat smiling?'

'Because it's a Cheshire Cat, that's why,' said the Duchess.

'So Cheshire Cats can smile. I didn't know that,' said Alice.

'You don't know much,' said the Duchess.

'That's not very polite,' thought Alice.

She started to say something. Suddenly, the cook threw a plate at the Duchess. The Duchess didn't move. The cook threw more things – plates, cups, spoons. Some of them hit the Duchess and the baby. The Duchess did nothing, but the baby started to cry. 'Oh, don't throw things at the baby!' cried Alice. 'You'll hit its pretty nose!'

'You be quiet, it isn't your baby!' the Duchess shouted. She began to sing to it. These were the words of the song:

Be angry with your little boy,
And hit him when he cries:
He has to know that he's a child,
He's really not your size!

The cook sang the song too. When they finished, they sang it again. The Duchess started to throw the baby up and down. At the end of the song, she threw the baby to Alice.

'Here, you can have it now,' she said. 'I have to get ready. I'm going to see the Queen.'

The cook threw another plate at the Duchess. It didn't hit her, but she left the room quickly.

◆

Alice looked at the baby. It was a strange little thing and not very pretty. She took it outside. 'I'll have to take this child away from here, or they'll kill it!' she thought. The baby made a strange little sound and she looked at it again.

'Its nose is changing!' she cried. She looked at it very carefully. 'Its face is changing, everything is changing! Oh! It's not a baby any more, it's a pig!'

It was *very* strange, but the baby was now a pig.

'What am I going to do with it?' Alice thought. The pig made another, louder sound. Alice put the little animal down and it ran happily away into the wood.

'It wasn't a pretty baby, but it's quite a pretty pig,' thought Alice.

◆

She looked round her and jumped. The Cheshire Cat was up in one of the trees. The Cat smiled at Alice.

'It looks kind, but perhaps it will get angry. They all get angry in this place,' thought Alice. So she spoke to it very politely. 'Cheshire Cat, dear,' she said.

The Cat's smile got bigger.

'Please, can you help me? I want to go somewhere new,' said Alice.

'Where do you want to go?' asked the Cat.

'Somewhere different,' Alice said.

'Somewhere different,' repeated the Cat. It thought for a minute or two. Then it said, 'Walk *that* way and you'll come to a house. A man lives there. He makes hats and he's very strange. We call him the "Mad Hatter".'

'But I don't want to meet a strange man,' said Alice.

The cat didn't answer her. It said, 'Walk this way and you'll find the March Hare. He's strange too.'

'But I told you, I don't want to meet strange animals.'

'Oh, you can't help that,' said the cat. 'We're all strange here. I'm strange. You're strange.'

'How do you know I'm strange?' asked Alice.

'Of course you are,' the Cat said. 'Everybody's strange here. I'm *very* strange. I laugh when I'm sad, and I cry when I'm happy. That's strange. Are you going to see the Queen today? She's quite strange too.'

'I'd like to see the Queen,' Alice said, 'but I haven't got an invitation.'

'You'll see me in the Queen's garden,' said the Cheshire Cat, and vanished.

◆

'That's strange, but not *very* strange,' thought Alice. She waited for two minutes, and the Cat came back again.

'What happened to the baby?' it asked.

'It changed into a pig,' Alice said.

'I knew it!' said the Cat and vanished again.

Alice stayed under the tree for a short time. 'Perhaps it will come back again,' she thought. But it didn't.

'I think I'll go and visit the March Hare,' said Alice. She started to walk to his home. After some minutes, she heard a sound. She looked up, and there was the Cheshire Cat in a tree – a different tree.

'Did you say "pig"?' asked the Cat.

'Yes,' Alice answered. Then she said, 'Cheshire Cat, one minute you vanish and the next minute you're there again. I don't like it.'

'I know,' said the cat. And this time it vanished quite slowly. First its body went, then its legs. Then all of it vanished, and there was only its smile.

'There are a lot of cats without a smile, but a smile without a cat! Now that's *very* strange!' Alice said.

'We're all strange here. I'm strange. You're strange.'

Slowly, the Cheshire Cat's smile vanished too, and Alice began to walk again. She saw the March Hare's house through the trees. It was bigger than the Duchess's house.

Alice ate some of the white mushrooms. She got bigger again. In a short time she was about 60 centimetres high. She felt afraid, but walked to the house.

'I hope the March Hare isn't *too* strange,' she thought.

Chapter 7   A Tea Party

There was a tree in front of the house. Under the tree was a big table with a lot of chairs round it. But there were only three at the table: the Mad Hatter, the March Hare and a large brown mouse. The Mouse sat between the Mad Hatter and the March Hare. It was asleep, so they talked over its head.

When they saw Alice, they cried, 'No, no, you can't sit here! There isn't a place for you!'

'There are a lot of places,' Alice said. She sat down in a chair at one end of the table.

'Have some wine,' the Mad Hatter said politely.

Alice looked round the table but there was only tea.

'I don't see any wine,' she answered.

'There isn't any,' said the March Hare.

'Then why did you say, "Have some wine"? It wasn't very polite of you,' Alice said angrily.

'We didn't invite you to tea, but you came. That wasn't very polite of *you*,' said the March Hare.

'No, it wasn't. Cut your hair!' said the Mad Hatter.

'Oh, be quiet,' said Alice.

The Mad Hatter opened his eyes very wide, but he said nothing. Then he took out his watch and looked at it. 'What day is it?' he asked.

Alice thought for a little. 'Wednesday, I think,' she said.

'My watch says Monday,' the Mad Hatter said. 'You see, I was right. Butter isn't good for a watch.' He looked angrily at the March Hare.

'But it was the *best* butter,' answered the March Hare.

'Yes, but you put it in with the bread knife. Perhaps some bread got in.'

The March Hare took the watch from the Mad Hatter and looked at it sadly. Then he put it in his tea. He took it out and looked at it again. 'It was the *best* butter, you know,' he repeated.

Alice looked at the watch. 'It's a strange watch!' she said. 'It tells you the day, but it doesn't tell you the time.'

'So? Does your watch tell you the year?' asked the Mad Hatter.

'No,' Alice answered, 'but it's the same year for a very long time.'

'And my watch doesn't tell the time because it's always tea-time.'

'Have some wine,' the Mad Hatter said politely.

Alice thought about that. 'I don't really understand you,' she said politely. She looked round the table. There were a lot of teacups on the table.

'We move from place to place,' said the Mad Hatter.

'Don't you wash the cups?' asked Alice.

'No, we don't have time,' said the Mad Hatter.

'Why not?' asked Alice.

'It's a long story,' said the Mad Hatter. 'Time was my friend, you see. But he and I aren't friends now. So he doesn't do anything for me. And I don't have time for anything.'

'I see,' said Alice and smiled politely. But she didn't really understand.

◆

'Oh, look! The Mouse is asleep again,' said the Mad Hatter. He took his teacup and put a little hot tea on the Mouse's nose. It woke up and started to sing.

'Be quiet!' the Mad Hatter said very loudly, and the Mouse stopped singing.

'Have some more tea,' the March Hare said to Alice.

'Thank you, but I haven't *got* any tea. So how can I have some more?'

'You *can* have more,' the Mad Hatter said. 'You can have more than nothing.'

'I don't think – ' Alice began.

'Then don't speak,' the Mad Hatter said.

Alice got up angrily and walked away from the table into the woods.

'Perhaps they'll call me back,' she thought. 'And then they'll be nice to me and give me some tea and bread-and-butter.'

But they didn't say anything.

When she looked back, the Mouse was asleep with its head on its plate.

'I'll never go *there* again,' Alice said. 'That was a stupid tea party!'

◆

She looked round and saw a door in one of the trees. 'A door in a tree? That's strange!' she thought. And she opened the door and went inside.

'Oh, good!' she cried. She was back in the long room, near the little table! 'I'm small now. I can get through the little door into the garden.'

The key was on the table. She took it and opened the little door. Then she ate some of the brown mushroom. She started to get smaller. When she was about 30 centimetres high, she walked through the door into the garden.

Chapter 8   Inside the Garden

Near Alice was a small tree with flowers on it. There were three gardeners by the tree.

'Be careful, Five!' one of them said.

'I'm *always* careful, Seven,' answered Five.

Alice went to them. 'What are you doing?' she asked.

'We're making the flowers red,' one of the gardeners said.

'That's strange!' thought Alice. 'Why?' she asked.

The three men looked unhappy.

'You tell her, Seven,' Five said.

'No,' said Seven, 'You tell her, Two.'

'Well, Miss, the Queen wanted trees with red flowers on them. But this tree's got white flowers! We don't want the Queen to see it. She'll be very angry and cut off our heads. So we're making the flowers red before she sees them.'

'Oh no!' Five shouted suddenly. 'The Queen! The Queen!'

'I'm always *careful, Seven,'* answered Five.

The three gardeners fell to the ground, with their faces down. Alice heard the sound of many feet and turned round.

'Oh good!' she thought. 'Now I'll see the Queen.'

♦

First, ten men with clubs in their hands came into the garden. Next came the King's men. There were ten of them, and they had red diamonds on their clothes. The children of the King and Queen came next, all with red hearts. After them there were a lot more people. Most of them were Kings and Queens. The White Rabbit was there, but he didn't see Alice. The Knave of Hearts came next. Last of all were the King and Queen of Hearts.

When these people saw Alice, they all stopped. The Queen said to the Knave of Hearts, 'Who is this?'

The Knave of Hearts didn't know. So he smiled and said nothing.

'Stupid man!' shouted the Queen. She turned to Alice and said, 'What's your name, child?'

'My name is Alice, Madam,' Alice answered.

She didn't feel very afraid of the Queen. 'They're only *cards*,' she thought.

The Queen looked at the gardeners. They were on the ground and she couldn't see their faces. 'Who are these men?' she asked.

'Don't ask *me*! I don't know,' answered Alice, not very politely.

The Queen's face got redder and redder. She looked at Alice and shouted, 'Cut off her head! Cut –'

'Oh, be quiet!' said Alice.

The Queen stopped shouting. The King put his hand on her arm. He said quietly, 'Don't be angry, my dear. She's only a child.'

The Queen turned away from him angrily. 'Turn those men over!' she said to the Knave of Hearts. The Knave did this very carefully, with one foot.

'Get up!' the Queen shouted.

She looked at Alice and shouted, 'Cut off her head!'

The three gardeners jumped up. The Queen turned to the little tree and looked at it carefully. 'What's wrong with these flowers?' she asked the gardeners.

'Well, you see, M – M – Madam,' said Two. 'They were white, and – and –'

The Queen looked from the flowers to the men. 'I see,' she said. 'Cut off their heads!'

Everybody started walking again. The gardeners ran to Alice. 'Help us!' they cried. Alice put them behind some trees.

'Don't be afraid,' she said. 'They're not going to cut off your heads.'

The King's men looked for the gardeners but couldn't find them. 'Are their heads off?' shouted the Queen.

'Yes, Madam,' shouted the King's men.

'Good!' shouted the Queen.

◆

Everybody started walking again and Alice walked with them.

'It's a very fine day,' somebody said. Alice turned round and there was the White Rabbit next to her.

'Very,' said Alice. 'Where's the Duchess?'

'Quiet!' said the Rabbit and looked all round him. Then he put his mouth near to Alice's ear. 'They're going to cut off her head!' he said.

'Why?' asked Alice.

'Did you say, "Oh no!"?' asked the White Rabbit.

'No, I didn't. I said, "Why?"'

'She hit the Queen,' the Rabbit said. Alice started to laugh.

'Quiet!' said the Rabbit again. 'The Queen will hear you, she hears everything. You see, the Duchess came late. When she arrived, the Queen said –'

Suddenly, the Queen shouted very loudly, 'Cut off their heads!'

'Who's going to lose their head now?' Alice wondered. She

began to feel afraid. 'The Queen isn't angry with me now,' she thought. 'But it will happen. I *would* like to speak to somebody about it.'

◆

She looked round. The White Rabbit wasn't there. She looked up. There was something above her head.

'What is it?' she wondered. She watched for a minute or two. It was a smile! 'It's the Cheshire Cat,' she thought. 'Now I can talk to somebody.'

'How are you?' the Cheshire Cat asked.

Alice waited. She thought, 'I won't speak to it before it has its ears – or perhaps one ear.'

In another minute, she could see its ears and eyes.

'Do you like the Queen?' the Cat asked.

'I don't,' said Alice. But then she saw the Queen. She was very near Alice. 'She's wonderful,' said Alice. The Queen smiled and moved away. But the King saw the Cat's head and came to Alice.

'Who *are* you talking to?' he asked.

'It's a friend – a Cheshire Cat,' answered Alice.

The King looked carefully at the Cat. 'I don't like it,' said the King.

'Well, *I* don't like *you*,' said the Cat.

'That's not polite,' said the King and got behind Alice.

Alice said, 'A cat can look at a King. I read that in a book, I think.'

'Well, this cat has to go,' said the King. He called to the Queen, 'My dear, I don't like this cat.'

The Queen had only one answer to problems. 'Cut off its head!' she shouted loudly. She didn't look at the Cat. The King smiled happily.

◆

After a short time, there were a lot of people round the Cat. There was the King and Queen, and a man with a very long knife in his hand.

'How can I cut off its head?' asked the man with the knife. 'I can't do it and I'm not going to.'

'Oh yes you are,' said the King. 'It's got a head, so you can cut it off.'

'Do something now, or I'll cut off everybody's head!' said the Queen angrily.

'What do you think?' the King asked Alice.

Alice thought for a minute. Then she said, 'It's the Duchess's Cat. Ask her about it.'

'Bring the Duchess here,' the Queen said.

Then the Cheshire Cat's head started to vanish. Somebody came back with the Duchess. But now there was nothing above Alice's head – not an eye or an ear or a smile. The King looked for the Cat for some time, but he couldn't find it anywhere.

◆

'Come for a walk, you dear thing,' the Duchess said to Alice. She put her arm through Alice's and they walked through the garden.

'She's very friendly to me,' thought Alice. 'Perhaps when the cook isn't there, she's nice. When *I'm* a Duchess, I'm going to be *kind* to my children.'

'Are you *thinking*?' asked the Duchess. 'You have to talk to me, you know.'

'All right,' said Alice. She could hear the Queen at the other end of the garden. 'Cut off her head! Cut off his head!' she shouted, every two or three minutes.

'Will they cut off *your* head?' Alice asked the Duchess.

'Oh no, they never cut off anybody's head. The Queen likes saying it, but she never does it.'

Alice wanted to ask more questions but they heard a cry: 'The trial is beginning!'

'What trial is it?' Alice asked. The Duchess didn't answer and started to run. Her arm was in Alice's, so Alice ran too.

Chapter 9   Who Took the Tarts?

Alice and the Duchess followed everybody into a house with one very large room. The King and Queen were there. They sat on big chairs above all the animals and birds. All the cards were there too. Near the King was the White Rabbit. He had a paper in his hand and looked very important. The Knave of Hearts stood in front of the King and Queen. He stood between two men and his head was down. It was his trial. In the middle of the room was a table with a large plate of tarts on it.

Alice found a place and sat down. She looked round.

'I know a lot of the animals and birds here,' she thought. She looked hungrily at the tarts.

'I hope they finish the trial quickly,' she thought. 'Then we can eat the tarts.'

Suddenly, the White Rabbit cried, 'Quiet please!'

The King looked round the room. 'Read the paper!' he said. The White Rabbit stood up and read from a very long paper:

The Queen of Hearts, she made some tarts,
One lovely sunny day;
The Knave of Hearts, he took those tarts,
He took them all away.

'Cut off his head!' cried the Queen.

'No, no,' said the Rabbit. 'We have to call people into the room, and ask them questions.'

'All right then. Call the Mad Hatter!' said the King.

The White Rabbit stood up and read from a very long paper.

The Mad Hatter came into the room. He had a teacup in one hand, and some bread-and-butter in the other hand.

'Why did you call me? I wanted to finish my tea,' he said.

'When did you begin your tea?' asked the King.

The Mad Hatter thought for a minute. The March Hare and the Mouse were quite near him and he looked at them for ideas. Then he said, 'March the fourteenth – I think.'

'Fifteenth,' said the March Hare.

'Sixteenth,' said the Mouse.

'Write that down,' said the King to the White Rabbit. Then he said to the Mad Hatter, 'Take off your hat.'

'It isn't mine,' said the Mad Hatter.

'Oh, so you took it from somebody, you bad man,' said the King.

'No, no! I *sell* hats. I'm a Hatter,' answered the Mad Hatter. He looked very afraid.

'Don't be afraid or I'll cut off your head!' said the King.

'I'm not a bad man!' the Mad Hatter cried. 'But the March Hare told me –'

'I didn't!' the March Hare said quickly.

'Well, the Mouse said ...' The Mad Hatter stopped and looked at the Mouse. But the Mouse didn't say anything, because he was asleep.

'After that,' said the Mad Hatter, 'I cut some more bread-and-butter.'

'But what did the Mouse say?' asked the King.

'I can't remember,' the Mad Hatter said.

'You have to remember,' the King said, 'or I'll cut off your head.'

'I'm a good man, Sir ...' the unhappy Mad Hatter began. But the King wasn't interested now.

'You can go,' he said to the Mad Hatter.

The Mad Hatter ran out of the room.

'Take his head off outside!' shouted the Queen. Two men ran after him. But the Mad Hatter ran very fast and they could not catch him.

◆

Alice did not feel very well. 'What's wrong with me?' she wondered. And then she understood. 'I'm getting bigger again,' she thought.

She was between the Duchess and the Mouse. 'You're hurting me,' the Duchess said.

'I can't do anything,' said Alice. 'I'm getting bigger.'

'You can't get bigger *here*,' said the Mouse.

'Yes, I can,' said Alice. 'You're getting bigger too.'

'Yes, but not as fast as you,' said the Mouse. He got up and sat in a different place.

'Call the next person!' said the King.

The next person came in. It was the Duchess's cook.

The King looked at her. 'What do you know about these tarts?' he asked. The cook didn't answer.

'Speak!' said the King.

'No!' said the cook.

'Ask her some questions,' the White Rabbit said to the King.

'All right, all right,' said the King. 'What was in those tarts?'

'Fish,' said the cook.

'Don't be stupid,' said the King. 'Call the next person!'

Alice looked round. 'Who can it be?' she wondered.

The White Rabbit looked at his paper and read the next name: 'Alice!'

Chapter 10   The End of the Trial

'Here!' cried Alice and stood up quickly. But she was tall now, and chairs, tables and people fell here, there and everywhere.

'Put everything and everybody back!' said the King loudly. Alice put them all back in their places. Then the King asked, 'What do you know about these tarts?'

'Nothing,' answered Alice.

'That's very important,' said the King.

'You mean, unimportant, Sir,' said the White Rabbit.

'Unimportant – of course,' said the King. 'Important – unimportant – important – unimportant,' he repeated.

He looked at Alice carefully. He took a book and read from it. 'Alice is more than a kilometre high. So she has to leave the room!' he said.

'I'm not more than a kilometre high –'Alice began.

'You are,' said the King.

'More than two kilometres high,' said the Queen.

'Well, I'm not leaving this room,' said Alice.

The King's face went white.

'Cut off her head!' shouted the Queen. Nobody moved.

'You stupid woman,' said Alice. She was very large now and she wasn't afraid of anybody.

'Cut off her head!' shouted the Queen.

'Don't be stupid!' Alice said. 'Who's afraid of you? *I'm* not. You're only cards!'

The cards – all fifty-two of them – came down on top of Alice. She felt afraid and angry and started to fight them. Then she opened her eyes . . .

◆

She saw a tree, a big old tree. She was under it, next to her sister. Her sister's hand was on her hair.

The cards came down on top of Alice.

'Wake up, Alice dear,' her sister said. 'You slept for a long time!'

'Oh!' said Alice, and then she understood. She sat up and told her sister about the White Rabbit and the rabbit-hole. When she finished her story, her sister laughed.

'Let's go home to tea,' she said. 'It's getting late.'

'Oh yes! I'd like some tea!' cried Alice. And she got up and ran home.

ACTIVITIES

Chapters 1–2

Before you read

1 Look at the Word List at the back of the book. The words are all in the story.

    a Which five words are for animals?

    b Which other things can you eat?

    c Which word do you use for the size of something?

    d What do you use when you open the door to your house?

2 Read the Introduction to the book. How is Wonderland different from our world?

While you read

3 Put one word into each sentence.

    a The White Rabbit takes a .... from its jacket.

    b Alice falls very .... down the rabbit hole.

    c There are four .... in the long room.

    d Alice sees a beautiful .... through the small door.

    e Alice finds a key and a .... on the table.

    f The drink makes Alice ....

    g The cake makes Alice ....

    h In a short time, Alice is .... than three metres high.

    i Alice gets .... again because she has the White Rabbit's hat in her hand.

4 Answer each question with Yes or No.

    a Is the White Rabbit afraid of the Duchess? .....

    b Is Alice afraid of the White Rabbit? .....

    c Does Alice fall into the sea? .....

    d Is the Mouse angry with Alice? .....

    e Are there other people in the water? .....

    f Do Alice and the Mouse get out of the water? .....

After you read

5 Discuss these questions.

    a What do you know now about Wonderland?

    b Alice fell down the rabbit-hole and arrived in Wonderland. How do you think she will get home again?

6 Work with two other students. Have this conversation.

    Student A: You are Alice. Ask the White Rabbit and the Mouse questions. Then answer their questions.

    Student B: You are the White Rabbit. Answer Alice's questions. Then ask her questions.

    Student C: You are the Mouse. Answer Alice's questions. Then ask her questions.

Chapters 3–4

Before you read

7 Look at the picture on page 8. What is strange about the bird with Alice?

8 When the animals and birds climb out of the water, they are cold and wet. How can they get warm? Think of some ideas.

While you read

9 Who

    a doesn't have a chocolate? ....

    b wants Dinah? ....

    c wants a hat? ....

    d doesn't want to meet Mary Ann? ....

    e wants to get into the small room? ....

    f eats another cake? ....

    g can't catch Alice? ....

    h is sitting on a mushroom? ....

After you read

10 Which of these people and animals does Alice meet in Chapters 3 and 4? Write (✓) or (✗).

a Mary Ann   .....

b the White Rabbit   .....

c Dinah   .....

d the Dodo   .....

e Pat   .....

f the Mouse   .....

g the Duchess   .....

h the Caterpillar   .....

11 What do you know about the White Rabbit's house?

12 Answer these questions.

a What size is Alice at the end of Chapter 4?

b Why doesn't she like that?

c What is she going to eat now?

Chapters 5–6

Before you read

13 Work with another student. Have this conversation.

Student A: You are the Caterpillar. You are not polite. Ask Alice, 'Who are you?' When she answers, ask more questions.

Student B: You are Alice. Answer the Caterpillar's questions.

While you read

14 What happens first? Number these sentences, 1–8.

a The baby changes into a pig.   .....

b Alice eats the mushrooms.   .....

c Alice goes to the March Hare's house.   .....

d The Duchess throws the baby to Alice.   .....

e Alice meets the Cheshire Cat.   .....

f Alice repeats, 'You are old, Father William.' .....

g The Duchess and the cook sing to the baby.   .....

h Alice finds a little house in the woods.   .....

15 Are these sentences right (✓) or wrong (✗)?

    a The Caterpillar sits under a mushroom.   .....

    b Alice gets smaller after she eats the brown mushroom.   .....

    c The Cheshire Cat has a very big smile.   .....

    d The Duchess is going to see the Queen.   .....

    e The cook throws plates, cups and spoons at Alice.   .....

    f The Cheshire Cat vanishes.   .....

16 Discuss these questions.

    a Do you think Alice likes the people and animals in Wonderland? Why (not)?

    b Some very strange things happen in the Duchess's house. What do you think is the strangest?

Chapters 7–8

Before you read

17 Look at the pictures on pages 22 and 25. What do you think is happening? Why is it happening?

While you read

18 Who says these things?

    a 'I don't see any wine.'   ....

    b 'Cut your hair!'   ....

    c 'My watch says Monday.'   ....

    d 'It was the best butter.'   ....

    e 'Have some more tea.'   ....

    f 'That was a stupid tea party.'   ....

19 Finish each sentence. Find the second half on page 43.

    a 'We're making the flowers red   .....

    b The three gardeners fell to the ground, ...

    c The Queen turned to the little tree   .....

    d The King's men looked for the gardeners   .....

    e Everybody started walking again   .....

    f The King looked for the Cat for some time   .....

g The Queen likes saying it, ...

h Her arm was in Alice's, ...

    1 and Alice walked with them.

    2 and looked at it carefully.

    3 but he couldn't find it anywhere.

    4 with their faces down.

    5 but she never does it.

    6 so Alice ran too.

    7 before she sees them.'

    8 but couldn't find them.

After you read

20 Discuss these questions.

    a Alice thinks the Mad Hatter's tea party is stupid. Why? What do you think?

    b Which people or animals are most friendly to Alice? Which are unfriendly?

Chapters 9–10

Before you read

21 Discuss these questions.

    a What do you think the trial is for?

    b What do you think will happen at the trial?

While you read

22 Who is the King talking to when he says these words at the trial?

    a 'Read the paper!' ....

    b 'When did you begin your tea?' ....

    c 'Write that down.' ....

    d 'Take off your hat.' ....

    e 'But what did the Mouse say?' ....

    f 'What do you know about these tarts?' ....

After you read

23 Where are all these people at the trial? Use these words:
in front of above in the middle of near between
  a The King and Queen are sitting on chairs ..... all the animals.
  b The White Rabbit is ..... the King.
  c The Knave of Hearts is standing ..... the King and Queen.
  d The Knave of Hearts is standing ..... two men.
  e The March Hare and the Mouse are quite ..... the Mad Hatter.
  f Alice is ..... the Duchess and the Mouse.
  g The tarts are ..... the room.
24 How does Alice leave Wonderland? What happens after she leaves? What does she do after she leaves? Discuss these questions.

Writing

25 Write three or four sentences about each of these animals or people:
  The White Rabbit   The Queen
  The Cheshire Cat   The Duchess
26 Which chapter in the book did you like best? Why? Write about it.
27 Write a short letter from Alice to a friend about Wonderland.
28 Write about one of the pictures in the book. What is happening? What happened before this? What is going to happen?
29 Alice leaves the tea party but the Mad Hatter, the March Hare and the Mouse stay at the table. They talk about Alice. Write their conversation.
30 Alice and her sister go home for tea. Alice is going to tell her mother about the Mad Hatter's tea party. Write her words to her mother.
31 Which person or animal in this story is the funniest? Why? Write about him, her or it.
32 What will you say about *Alice in Wonderland* to your friends? Do you think they will enjoy it? Why (not)? Write about the book.

Answers for the Activities in this book are available from the Pearson English Readers website.
A free Activity Worksheet is also available from the website. Activity worksheets are
part of the Pearson English Readers Teacher Support Programme, which also includes
Progress tests and Graded Reader Guidelines. For more information, please visit:
www.pearsonenglishreaders.com

WORD LIST *with example sentences*

body (n) He washed his face and *body* in the river.

caterpillar (n) There are green *caterpillars* on the flowers.

centimetre (n) How many *centimetres* are there in a metre?

duchess (n) Charles's wife, Camilla, is the *Duchess* of Cornwall.

hare (n) He caught a *hare* and cooked it for dinner.

hole (n) There is a *hole* in the door. One of the boys put his foot through it.

key (n) Can I have the *key* to the front door? I can't get into the house.

land (n) I'm British. My parents came to this *land* before I was born.

mad (adj) You can't go on holiday without any money! Are you *mad*?

mouse (n) I hear *mice* in the kitchen at night, but I never see them.

mushroom (n) Would you like *mushrooms* with your eggs?

pig (n) We had two *pigs*, but we sold them for meat.

polite (adj) Don't take the last cake! It isn't *polite*.

rabbit (n) Last year *rabbits* ate the vegetables in our garden.

race (n) I lost the *race* because my leg hurt.

tart (n) Let's eat these fruit *tarts* with our tea.

tear (n) She cried, and *tears* ran down her face.

trial (n) They say that he killed a policewoman. His *trial* starts next week.

vanish (v) She was in front of me – and then she *vanished*!

wonder (n/v) Disneyland is a children's *wonderland*.

'What did I do wrong?' he *wondered*.

Better learning
comes from fun.

Pearson English **Readers**

There are plenty of Pearson English Readers to choose from
- world classics, film and television adaptations, short stories, thrillers,
modern-day crime and adventure, biographies, American classics,
non-fiction, plays ... and more to come.

For a complete list of all Pearson English Readers titles, please contact
your local Pearson Education office or visit the website.

pearsonenglishreaders.com

Notes:

Notes:

Notes:

LONGMAN
Dictionaries

Express yourself with confidence

Longman has led the way in ELT dictionaries since 1935. We constantly talk to students and teachers around the world to find out what they need from a learners' dictionary.

Why choose a Longman dictionary?

EASY TO UNDERSTAND

Longman invented the Defining Vocabulary - 2000 of the most common words which are used to write the definitions in our dictionaries. So Longman definitions are always clear and easy to understand.

REAL, NATURAL ENGLISH

All Longman dictionaries contain natural examples taken from real-life that help explain the meaning of a word and show you how to use it in context.

AVOID COMMON MISTAKES

Longman dictionaries are written specially for learners, and we make sure that you get all the help you need to avoid common mistakes. We analyse typical learners' mistakes and include notes on how to avoid them.

DIGITAL INNOVATION

Longman dictionaries are also available online at:
www.longmandictionaries.com or **www.longmandictionariesusa.com**

These are premier dictionary websites that allow you to access the best of Longman Learners' dictionaries, whatever you do, wherever you are. They offer a wealth of additional resources for teachers and students in the Teacher's Corner and the Study Centre.